Big Words
for Little People

by Donna Lugg Pape
illustrated by Lorraine Arthur

Compassion
Politeness
Kindness
Patience

Third Edition, 1996
Library of Congress Catalog Card Number 84-052168
© 1985, The Standard Publishing Company, Cincinnati, Ohio
A division of Standex International Corporation. Printed in U.S.A.

Compassion is a big word for little people. It is something to have that makes a little person BIG. It is a way of being and a way of doing to show that you care.

Compassion is being extra kind to your friend when he is sad about something.

Compassion is not calling names even though everyone else is.

Compassion is being a friend when someone
needs one.

Compassion is a big word with a big meaning. It can be owned by everyone, even little people. Grown-ups say it comes from the heart.

Politeness can be shown every day in many ways. When someone gives you a present, you can show politeness by saying, "Thank you."

When you want your father to help you, you can show politeness by saying, "Please."

Politeness is saying, "You're welcome," to a friend after she thanks you for something.

Politeness is saying, "Excuse me," if you bump into someone while you are running.

You can show politeness
if you give your seat
on a bus
to a grandma or grandpa
who has to stand.

...ndness can be shown in things we say or do not say. It can be shown in things we do or do not do every day.

Kindness is helping Father put the nest back in the tree if it has fallen to the ground.

Kindness is stopping to help a small person in trouble, even though you are in a big, big hurry.

Kindness can be helping someone on his tri-cycle if he has taken a tumble.

Kindness can be wiping off the tears of someone who has hurt himself and taking him home to his mother if it is a big hurt.

Kindness is visiting a lonely grandmother or grandfather who lives next door.

Kindness is not staring at someone who is different, but giving her a smile.

Patience is a quiet thing—something that
can grow every day in little ways.

Patience is waiting for a baby kitten to grow big enough for you to take it home.

Patience is turning an end of the skipping rope instead of being the one to jump.

Patience is waiting quietly to tell Mother something until she is finished talking to Father.

Patience is trying again and again when learning something new until something hard becomes easy to do.

If you try to show compassion, politeness, kindness, and patience, you are being the kind of you God wants you to be.